MW01714434

In The Image and Likeness of God: A Hope-Filled Anthropology

Published by the Anglican Consultative Council
16 Tavistock Crescent
London W11 1AP, UK
ISBN 978-1-911007-02-9

 Set in Adobe Caslon Pro 12/18.

In The Image and Likeness of God: A Hope-Filled Anthropology

The Buffalo Statement

Agreed by the International Commission for Anglican-Orthodox Theological Dialogue

2015

Published by the Anglican Communion Office

Contents

Preface by the Co-Chairs of the Dialogue

The Buffalo Agreed Statement is the fourth such document to be endorsed by the International Commission for Anglican–Orthodox Theological Dialogue (ICAOTD). The dialogue commenced its work at Oxford in 1973. The first two agreed statements, endorsed at Moscow in 1976 and at Dublin in 1984, covered a wide range of topics. *The Moscow Agreed Statement* considered the knowledge of God (the distinction between the divine essence and the divine energies), the inspiration and authority of the Holy Scripture, the relation between Scripture and Tradition, the authority of councils, the *Filioque* clause, the Church as Eucharistic community, and the invocation of the Holy Spirit in the Eucharist. *The Dublin Statement* discussed in general terms the mystery of the Church, faith in the Trinity, prayer and holiness, the communion of saints and the departed, and icons.

The third agreed statement, *The Church of the Triune God*, adopted at Cyprus in 2006, analysed more systematically and in far greater detail the theme of ecclesiology. It gave careful consideration to the understanding of the episcopate and the meaning of primacy and synodality, and to the variety of Christian ministries. In the section entitled 'Christ, Humanity, and the Church', *The Cyprus Statement* also raised questions concerning the Christian understanding of the human person.

Developing what was said on this subject in *The Cyprus Statement*, from 2009 onwards the Commission has concentrated upon the theme of Christian anthropology. This is particularly timely, in view of the wide-ranging developments in biotechnology and genetic engineering, and also in our appreciation of the human place in the universe, whose vast extent has become apparent to us in a way far beyond the imagination of earlier generations. We recognize that all of this, together with the far-ranging changes in attitudes within secular society concerning the place of God and the Church, has raised serious and fundamental difficulties for Christian theology.

We have planned a document in two parts. The first part, *In the Image and Likeness of God: A Hope-Filled Anthropology*, the document here submitted, sets out the primary doctrines held in common by our two communions. In the second part, yet to be drafted and agreed, we intend to indicate the practical consequences that follow from these theological presuppositions. Topics to be discussed will include the responsibility of humankind for the environment, questions on sexuality, the meaning of marriage, and human interventions at different stages of life: before and at birth (birth control, abortion, experimentation on the foetus, etc.), during the course of life (transplant of organs), and at death (euthanasia, assisted dying). All of these questions involve our understanding of human rights. Where appropriate, the Commission will seek advice from experts on these complex issues.

The meetings of the Commission have been marked by a spirit of warm friendship and by a continuing growth in mutual trust. Without any compromise on either side, we have so far reached a broad agreement on almost all points. A continuing difficulty since 1977 concerns the Anglican decision to ordain women to the priesthood and the episcopate; it is also possible that we shall not agree entirely concerning the practical consequences of our theology of personhood. Yet without doubt our recent dialogue is drawing us more closely together, as we share in the prayer of Christ: 'May they all be one.'

Metropolitan Kallistos of Diokleia, Ecumenical Patriarchate

Archbishop Roger Herft, Anglican Communion

Beginning with Praise

I praise you, for I am fearfully and wonderfully made.
Wonderful are your works;
that I know very well;
My frame was not hidden from you,
when I was being made in secret,
intricately woven in the depths of the earth.
Your eyes beheld my unformed substance.
In your book were written
all the days that were formed for me,
when none of them as yet existed.
How weighty to me are your thoughts, O God!
How vast is the sum of them!

Ps 139.14–17

He has told you, O mortal, what is good;
and what does the Lord require of you
but to do justice, and to love kindness,
and to walk humbly with your God?

Mic 6.8

From one ancestor he made all nations to inhabit the whole earth, and he allotted the times of their existence and the boundaries of the places where they would live, so that they would search for God and perhaps grope for him and find him—though indeed he is not far from each one of us. For 'in him we live and move and have our being'.

Acts 17.26–28a

Introduction: The Heavens are Telling the Glory of God

1. *Creation as a Gift of God: The God-Given Reality of the Human Person*

Orthodox and Anglicans, relying on Scripture and the common Christian tradition, understand the fundamental determining reality of the human person to be our relationship with the triune God. Creation, including humankind, is a gift of God, expressing his love and revealing the divine intention. In creation, God brings into existence human beings with the freedom to love both God and their fellow creatures. To be human is to know, love, and delight in God and to share in God's life as far as created beings may. Thus it is in praising and worshipping God that we discover who we are as human beings. In the Fall humans chose to live outside of the divine–human communion, bringing disharmony, suffering, and death into the world. Nevertheless, creation continues to reveal the divine intention, and through Christ God offers forgiveness and the renewal of all creation (Rom 1.20; 8.18–21).

2. *Authentic Relationship with God through Christ*

The full potential of the human person is revealed in Christ, by the Holy Spirit. In Christ we are brought face to face with the Father (Jn 14.9). In Christ, we are also enabled to face ourselves and one another as we truly are. God has become human not only that we may share in the divine life, but also that we may become fully human. St Athanasius said, 'He became human that we might be made divine.'[1] We could also affirm that He became human that we might be made truly human. Through the Incarnation, Crucifixion, Resurrection, and Ascension—and through the extension of these events in the sacramental life—all humanity, together with the whole of creation, is called to participate in God's saving action.

Both Anglicans and Orthodox describe the work of Christ by referring to him as the last Adam (1 Cor 15.45). Christ heals the wounds inflicted upon human nature and the whole creation through the transgression of the first Adam. Christ sums up and gathers in himself all creation (Eph 1.10): in the words of St Irenaeus of Lyons, 'As the eternal King, he recapitulates all things in Himself.'[2] Christ suffered on behalf of humankind to bring us to participation in the community of the triune God, triumphing over sin and evil and making 'peace through the blood of his cross' (Col 1.20). Thus we are a new creation (2 Cor 5.17), 'God's own people' (1 Pet 2.9), forgiven, healed, and renewed.

3. *Responding with Praise and Thanksgiving*

Creation is a divine work of art, a reflection of the glory of God. The Book of Genesis describes God as seeing creation as 'good and beautiful' (Gen 1.31–2.1 LXX). Humanity created in the image and likeness of God is blessed through grace to be a partner with the divine in the continuing work of creation. Frail dust though we are, with all our paradoxes and pathos, yet we are dust that dreams of glory; as St Irenaeus affirms: 'The glory of God is a human being fully alive.'[3] Just as we are called to share in God's work, we are called to share in God's Sabbath rest (Gen 2.2–3): this also is an expression of praise and thanksgiving.

By the power of the Spirit, humanity responds in praise to God's gift of creation. As beings that praise God together we participate in the divine life (2 Pet 1.4). The healing and restoration of creation by God are reflected in Christ. As members of the glorified Body of Christ—the Church—we worship in the Spirit while we actively await the fulfilment of the promises of the coming reign of God. 'Let the heavens praise your wonders, O Lord, your faithfulness in the assembly of the holy ones' (Ps 89.5). As is proclaimed in our Eucharistic prayers, Eastern and Western: 'Holy, holy, holy is the Lord of hosts; the whole earth is full of his glory' (Isa 6.3).

1. The Human Person within the Created Order

4. *Sources of Christian Anthropology*

Our understanding of the human person is based upon the joint witness of Scripture and Tradition. Employing the gifts of human reason and understanding, the Church uses the biblical sources of the Old and New Testaments as witness to God in Christ, as guides through the complexities of existence, and as models for addressing existential issues that face humanity in every generation. 'Any disjunction between Scripture and Tradition such as would treat them as two separate sources of revelation must be rejected. The two are correlative.'[4] Church life is in continuity with the prophetic and apostolic life of faith, and the Church with the guidance of the Holy Spirit (Jn 16.7, 13) interprets the biblical texts for every generation as new questions arise.

5. *Person as Mystery*

Every person, made in God's image, is inexhaustible in meaning: no delineation of our human characteristics can fully describe the depths of our personhood. We are each of us a mystery to ourselves and to one another. We approach this mystery of personhood with a sense of awe and wonder. 'Beloved, we are God's children now; what we will be has not yet been revealed' (1 Jn 3.2).

6. *Person as Relationship*

God reveals himself to us as a unity of three persons, sharing the same divine being in boundless love for one another. God the Father pre-eternally loves the only-begotten Son and issues forth the Holy Spirit, the Giver of Life and the Comforter. The *perichoresis* or mutual indwelling of the three persons of the Trinity is ultimately the source of all created unity and diversity, of its interweaving and mutual interdependence, of its ever-growing complexity. Human beings reflect this divine co-inherence through expressing with gratitude their own interrelationship and in emulating God's hospitality to what is other. Abraham and Sarah, in offering hospitality to three strangers, are in fact welcoming the presence of God himself (Gen 18.1–5). Human beings are inquisitive, probing, exploratory, delighting in diversity and in encountering new people and ideas. We are enabled to love one another in a Trinitarian way because God the Trinity has first loved us (1 Jn 4.7, 19).

7. *The Unique Value of Each Person*

Christian anthropology goes beyond a merely utilitarian approach to the human being. It is the light of the Logos (Jn 1.9) that makes every one of us Godlike and unique. All human beings, regardless of their situation or condition, are loved by God and are to be valued as true persons. Seeming weakness—even permanent disability or terminal illness—may contain strength of the highest order, where 'power is made perfect in weakness' (2 Cor 12.9). Indeed it is in apparent frailty that the uniqueness of human personhood may shine forth most strikingly, reaffirming itself in both those who give and those who receive loving care.

8. *Person as Sacrifice*

As the perfect image of God revealing the divine, Christ exemplifies the endless and unfathomable self-emptying of God: 'Let the same mind be in you that was in Christ Jesus, who, though he was in the form of God, did not regard equality with God as something to be exploited, but emptied himself … and became obedient to the point of death, even death on a cross. Therefore God also highly exalted him' (Phil 2.5–9). This self-emptying, which is also the fullness (*pleroma*) of divine love, is set before us as the ideal that we also should follow. Hence our capacity for interrelationship often involves 'self-emptying' (*kenosis*) and self-sacrifice, even the willingness to undergo martyrdom.

9. *The Human Person as Creative Co-Worker with God*

Our vocation as human persons is particularly affirmed by our capacity for conscious cooperation with God: we are fellow-workers (*synergoi*) with God (1 Cor 3.9). This is our chief glory. Protecting the dignity of all life, caring for the created order, and aspiring to holiness are essential manifestations of the true response of humankind to God's calling. Human capacity for freedom implies responsibility. We are called to view the created order as our fragile 'other', a subject rather than an object, in need of protection and creative and imaginative nurture. Approaching creation in love, as a gift to ourselves and others, both individuals and societies are challenged to actions of generous self-giving, frugality, and self-restraint.

As we come to understand our being as gift, and all creation as sustained by God, we also recognize our intrinsic limitations and fragility. This awareness calls us to forge stronger relationships with God and with one another. It is our task as human beings to ensure that the blessings of creation are distributed with justice among the nations. The struggle against poverty is both a material and a spiritual imperative.

10. *Human Freedom as Loving Obedience in Christ*

Made in the image of God who is supremely free, we humans express our uniqueness as persons through the exercise of free will. God gives us the capacity for freedom, both 'formal' freedom of choice between options, and 'substantial' freedom in and for God. Freedom, while a precious gift, can be used for good or for ill, involving as it does the possibility of choosing evil. The proper use of the gift of freedom is revealed in the person of Jesus Christ, who came to make us truly free (Jn 8.32, 36). Such freedom is given to us in order that we may participate fully in the rule of justice and holiness. The first step on this path is a fundamental change of mind, a far-reaching repentance (*metanoia*). The true dimension of freedom is found in loving obedience to God, 'whose service is perfect freedom'[5] (see Rom 6.17–18).

II . Image and Likeness

II. *The Created Image of the Uncreated God*

Human beings are created according to the image and likeness of God (Gen 1.26–27). In neither the Orthodox nor the Anglican tradition has any single interpretation of the significance of image and likeness been adopted as dogma. In general terms, however, we are agreed that each of us is a created image or 'icon' of the uncreated God. This entails a special position of the human being within the created order, given by God for the common good of all creation. Our humanity cannot be understood properly apart from our relationship with God. The human person created according to the image of God may be understood both Christologically and in a Trinitarian sense, signifying that we are both in the image of Christ the Divine Logos and in the image of the Holy Trinity.

In interpreting the divine image in Christological terms it is important to note that we are not created according to the image of a faceless, remote, or abstract God, but according to the image of the person of Christ. It is Christ himself who is 'the image of the invisible God, the firstborn of all creation' (Col 1.15), while we in our turn are 'according to the image' of Christ.

12. *Human Growth through the Gift of the Image and Likeness*

In the Christian tradition there are two ways of understanding the terms 'image' (*tselem*, *eikon*) and 'likeness' (*demuth*, *homoiosis*). Sometimes the two terms are understood as an example of Hebrew parallelism, so that the two denote the same reality: we are created with the quality of the divine running through us. They refer to the divine 'form' or potential stamped upon our nature as an integral whole.

Alternatively, a distinction is often made between the two terms. The image primarily implies the inherent capacity for rationality, freedom, and self-governance, while the likeness signifies the progressive actualization of this inherent capacity by living in accordance with the will and love of God. The ability to reflect God can be traced in all aspects of human life. Thus the image is what is given at the outset, conferred on all of us as persons, whereas the likeness is attained through our free cooperation (*synergeia*) with grace.

Just as God acts 'according to his counsel and will' (Eph 1.11), so too human beings seek to find appropriate maxims, rules, and procedures to govern their own actions. In this way they can address the pressing issues of their day, can support their families, and can work for the betterment of their societies and of the environment, for justice and peace. The capacity to do this is fundamental to human nature. To this end human beings are schooled, in both the humanities and the natural sciences, and in the religious teachings and traditions of their societies. All human beings, under God's grace, are involved in this process of growth and in this way enjoy the gifts of creation.

Through our dynamic growth we are conformed to the image of the Son of God (Rom 8.29), sharing ever more fully in deification (*theosis*). 'And all of us, with unveiled faces, seeing the glory of the Lord as though reflected in a mirror, are being transformed into the same image from one degree of glory to another' (2 Cor 3.18). In this way we participate in the mystery of Christ's transfiguration (Mt 17.2).

This dynamic growth, by the action of divine grace within us, is attained through repentance and prayer, through the sacramental life, and through the life of service in obedience to the commandments of Christ. The life of prayer is not limited to our conscious acts of prayer, but includes also the unceasing prayer of the Spirit within us (Rom 8.26), offered up in the midst of our weakness and exhaustion. All human prayer reflects the prayer of Jesus himself to his Father, and so fulfils the deepest dimension of human life formed in the image and likeness of God.

13. *The Virgin Mary: Perfection of Humanity by Grace*

The incarnate Christ is the perfect example of what it is to be fully human. Next after Christ and never apart from him, by his grace and mercy, the Virgin Mary, through her obedience and faith, is the highest example of what it means to be human. Like us she is saved through the incarnation and death of Christ. As 'birth-giver of God' (*Theotokos*) she is the one through whom God becomes human, so that human beings may become children of God.

The Blessed Virgin Mary is honoured by Orthodox and Anglicans alike as the definitive exemplar of responsive and dynamic discipleship for all humankind. At the Annunciation she is not a passive figure, but in full freedom, by a courageous act of choice, she accepts God's call as representative of the whole of humanity: 'let it be with me according to your word' (Lk 1.38). The Blessed Virgin proclaims in the *Magnificat* (Lk 1.46–55) that the promised reign of God's justice is breaking in upon the earth: 'he has filled the hungry with good things, and sent the rich away empty' (Lk 1.53). 'Do whatever he tells you' (Jn 2.5) are words of the Blessed Virgin to all generations, as she represents for us an archetype of the Church itself. She is seen as the second Eve, as Christ is the new Adam; in the words of the Akathist hymn, 'Rejoice, restoration of fallen Adam: Rejoice, redemption of the tears of Eve!'[6]

The Virgin Mary, who has been given a supreme dignity at the heart of the mystery of the Incarnation, is the glorious and glorified pattern of grace and hope for all humankind.[7] From an early date, Christians of East and West have believed that the Blessed Virgin Mary has already passed beyond death and judgement, entering into the eternal bliss that is promised in the Resurrection at the Last Day (but it is important to note that by no means all Anglicans hold this belief). She is a sign of the universal hope of Christian believers that they will share the new life of the Risen Christ.

14. *Free yet Fallen*

Even if image and likeness are distinguished, nevertheless they remain organically united in each living person. Among the essential, interrelated features of the human person are the following characteristics and capacities:

- ◊ God-awareness, prayer, worship, and adoration of the divine mystery;
- ◊ self-awareness, rationality, conscience, a sense of right and wrong;
- ◊ self-transcendence (*ekstasis*), the ability to reach out beyond ourselves to God and others in love;
- ◊ self-sacrifice as voluntary self-giving and self-emptying (*kenosis*) for the sake of the other;
- ◊ freedom and responsiveness, self-restraint and growth;

◊ self-expression as creativity and inspired imagination;
◊ responsibility for creation.

The divine image and likeness in the human person have been obscured through the Fall, but not obliterated. In other words, we are fallen yet not forlorn. We are indeed aware of being fallen at a deep level and of the far-reaching consequences of this fallenness: 'For I do not do the good I want' (Rom 7.19). Yet despite fallenness all human beings still possess freedom. To be human is to work with hope and self-criticism for truth and justice.

15. *In the Image of Both Logos and Trinity: Rationality and Discernment*

Since human persons are created according to the image of Christ the Divine Logos, they are endowed with the gift of rationality. This capacity for rationality is more than mere reason (*dianoia*) in the sense of logical analysis, important though this is. It includes also a higher capacity, the intellect (*nous*), which connotes an immediate discernment (*diakrisis*) of truth and beauty through inner vision: 'we have the mind (*nous*) of Christ'. (1 Cor 2.16) Through the *nous*, as well as through systematic analysis, we evaluate the spiritual worth of that which we analyse. Thus we become aware of both our intellectual and moral responsibility, of the 'common good', and of our freedom to act discerningly in the name of moral and spiritual values.

Our capacity for free discernment is double-edged. It may be used either in accordance with the divine will or against it. It is in this sense that we can understand the tree of the knowledge of good and evil (Gen 3.3). A self-imposed isolation from God—as epitomized by Adam in the Genesis narrative (Gen 3.8–9)—can lead only to a destructive alienation from God and from all that it means to be human. Our exercise of freedom and of *nous* is therefore not carried out in isolation. Human capacity for such freedom and *nous* means that we are always reaching out to what is other. This has both a horizontal and a vertical dimension: we reach out vertically to the Logos in whose image we are created, and horizontally to our brothers and sisters, according to the image of the Trinity. In Christ on the cross there is an intersection and integration of these vertical and horizontal dimensions. We seek the help of the Word and Spirit of God, made available to us through the sanctifying ministries and sacraments of his holy Church.

16. *Dominion, Stewardship, Priesthood*

In the Genesis account, the creation of humankind according to the image and likeness involves 'dominion' (Gen 1.28). However, this dominion is not to be understood as arbitrary and tyrannical domination. It is precisely a dominion according to the image of God himself, who is loving and compassionate. Thus the dominion with which we humans are entrusted signifies humility in self-giving service. We are called to heal, restore, and reconcile that which is fallen through our disobedience. We may be called stewards of creation, and this rightly emphasizes that the creation is not our private property but belongs to God (Ps 24.1). At the same time, this stewardship is not to be interpreted as implying that the created order is merely an asset to be exploited, to be treated as an *it* rather than a *thou*. Human beings have, therefore, a responsibility to care for the whole created order and to foster ecological justice. The best description, however, is to say that we humans are priests of the creation. It is the essence of priesthood to offer, and so we fulfil our true vocation as persons created according to the divine image when, exercising our royal priesthood (1 Pet 2.9), we offer the creation back to the Creator in joyful thanksgiving.

Our relationship to the created order is not static but dynamic. In Eden Adam did not simply admire the garden passively, but was commanded 'to till it and to keep it' (Gen 2.15). He fulfilled this active ministry in particular when he gave names to the animals (Gen 2.19–20), thus discerning the true value and intrinsic dignity of each creature, and so enhancing the harmony of meaning and beauty in the world of nature.

We recognize, however, that human beings have exploited the world's resources, that its gifts are unequally distributed, that the presence of hunger and food insecurity in large parts of the world is deeply disturbing. Human exploitation of the created order carries even larger implications. Whole ecological systems have been destroyed through human agency, and climate change on a global scale now appears all but irreversible. The responsibility conferred on us by our priesthood of the creation requires that all of us should acknowledge our complicity, and should struggle to overcome these distortions. This demands of us both our urgent attention and our effective action.

17. *Animals: Sentient and Sensitive, Deserving Care, Worthy of Respect*

God's love extends to all human persons regardless of ability, gender, ethnicity, and socio-economic or other status. But God's love extends yet further, repairing the torn fabric of the whole of creation.

Our relation to animal life is a part of our ecological care for the whole of creation. We continually encounter the living plenitude of our natural environment, which is integrally connected with the historical and social evolution of humankind. Nature is abundant with countless species of plant and animal life: 'O Lord, how manifold are your works! In wisdom you have made them all; the earth is full of your creatures ... These all look to you' (Ps 104.24–27). Although animals are not self-conscious persons they are alive and sentient, displaying the creative word and wisdom of God in their own ways. They have a beauty, playfulness, and value of their own.

Our close interdependence with the animals is evident in the way the Fall affects the created order in its entirety. Humankind is endangering and rendering extinct whole species of living creatures: 'the creation was subjected to futility, not of its own will' (Rom 8.19–20). Lamentably, animals have learned to fear human beings and often react with aggressive behaviour. Yet animals may also sense human goodness when it is present. The holy fathers and mothers of the Church mirror the selfless way of Christ's humble love for all beings. St Gerasimos of the Jordan, St Melangell of Wales, St Francis of Assisi, or St Seraphim of Sarov, to take but a few examples, established uncanny and astonishing relations to what is seemingly wild or untamed animal life. Such saints thus demonstrate the transformative power of life in God's grace. They call us to extend our respect for the dignity of all created life, including the animal and plant kingdom. 'Ever since the creation of the world his eternal power and divine nature, invisible though they are, have been understood and seen through the things he has made' (Rom 1.20).

It is true that in Christian tradition, both Eastern and Western, as in Judaism, it has been considered legitimate for humans to kill animals, so long as this is done humanely and not wantonly, and to use them for food. At the same time, there are those who prefer not to eat animals. Whatever the choice made here, as Christians we agree that animals have a specific worth of their own and are never to be treated with cruelty.

The tradition of the Church teaches us that we govern the created order properly only if we are able and willing to render it service in God's name. In this we follow the example of Christ, subjecting ourselves to the will of God.

Jesus Christ calls us to heal and restore creation as a whole, working together with God (2 Cor 6.1). When Jesus prayed that we might be taken up into the unity that exists between himself and the Father (Jn 17.21–23), this should be understood as implying the inclusion of the whole of creation. Hope for creation is to be regarded in cosmic terms: 'creation itself will be set free from its bondage to decay and will obtain the freedom of the glory of the children of God' (Rom 8.21).

18. *Divine Revelation and Human Creativity:* Logos *and* Logoi

Divine revelation and human creativity are interconnected. Revelation is universal and accessible to all. The created order may be understood as imbued with God's dynamic presence in the form of the divine *logoi*: in the words of St Maximus the Confessor, 'all created things are defined, in their essence and in their way of developing, by their own *logoi*'.[8] The *logoi* express the creative will of God, the divine intention in relation to each created being. All the divine *logoi* have their source in the one Logos of God and find their true end in him. In this way, the created order is to be understood as logical, dynamically structured, open, meaningful, and alive. Our capacity for creativity reflects the divine act of creation. The human mind, free yet fallen, can be attuned to the world around us in a fruitful way, yet it can also be used sinfully for destruction. As co-workers with God we participate in the ongoing, dynamic process of divine revelation and creation.

19. *God-Awareness in the Sciences and the Arts*

Our reasoning capacities, including our spiritual understanding, are given that we may be good custodians of creation and discover its potential through imaginative exploration, anticipative thinking, ethical evaluation, and responsible decision-making. We exercise this custodianship through scientific enquiry and technology, and likewise through the arts and philosophy.

The philosophy of science contends that fundamental scientific statements should be regarded as hypothetical working models having a conditional explanatory status, which as a matter of principle may be falsifiable. Theology has always recognized the inherent contingency of human enquiry as a created phenomenon, prone to error yet endowed with the ability through God's grace to overcome its shortcomings.

Despite this contingency, it can be affirmed with some confidence that the same underlying structures of nature are to be found across the galaxies, throughout the vastness of space, and across the millennia, throughout the full extent of time. One of the wonders of the universe is the way in which mathematicians construct models in their own mental worlds, and then find that the actual world bears out their speculations. Despite all limitations, our human image and likeness of the divine Logos reflect dynamically the deep grammar or patterning and the potential of all created being. It is precisely through human discovery that the sense of mystery deepens, and conversely, the sense of mystery invites more discovery as our wonder grows.

Many advances in science may be regarded as being of God's grace—rather than merely self-sufficient breakthroughs—allowing humankind to marvel at and benefit from the wealth of God's fullness. Max Planck rightly recognized the common purpose of science and faith: 'Religion and science are fighting a joint battle … against scepticism and against dogmatism, against disbelief and against superstition, and the rallying cry … has always been, and always will be: "On to God!" … Natural science wants us to learn, religion wants us to act!'[9]

We need to recognize, however, that because of our fallen nature everything in creation takes on a shadow of ambivalence. Science and technology can be used for ill as for good, and the history of the last century provides many examples of the abuse of technology and the scientific knowledge that lies behind it. The misuse of science can lead people away from God, and science can even become a god in itself. Deprived of the divine criteria of good and evil, science can lead to the dehumanization of persons and even the destruction of creation. Similarly the arts can also result in the dehumanization of the human person.

We stand in awe-filled wonder before the beauty of the created order. We recognize that God is revealed to us not only in truth and goodness but equally in beauty. 'The heavens are telling the glory of God; and the firmament proclaims his handiwork' (Ps 19.1). We also recognize the tension that exists between order and chaos within creation as we know it (Ps 107.23–30). The arts mirror the best and the worst of human experience. Creativity in all its diversity of cultural forms expresses the human response to this tension, through artistry and deep reflection and engagement. In all the arts—in, for example, Bach's Mass in B Minor or Rublev's icon of the Holy Trinity—we discover the breathtaking array of possibilities for displaying, rearranging, and discovering the meaning of created life. In the rhythms of chant, in the interplay of form, movement, and colour, in arresting juxtapositions of images and words, the arts are not only places where we may engage truthfully and profoundly with the world we inhabit; they may lead us to a deeper life of praise and wonder before the Creator.

20. *Against Idolatry*

Any approach to the full range of human activity, including science and the arts, presupposes our capacity to relate primarily in love to God, the source of all creation. Human beings are tempted to worship the created order rather than the Creator (Rom 1.23). The sin of idolatry establishes a creature as a false god at the cost of losing the personal relation to God and others. This self-enclosed approach to humanity tends to treat others simply as depersonalized individuals, as physical objects, or as resources.

We are truly who we are only if we relate to others as persons created according to the image of God, and if we view the freedom and uniqueness of others as expressions of divine gift. More concretely, we are called to offer ourselves on behalf of others in humble and sacrificial service as Christ did. Only in such a case, when self-interest is sacrificed, does human communion transcend both collectivism and individualism: 'We, who are many, are one body in Christ, and individually we are members one of another' (Rom 12.5). We receive life from God through our parents and through companionship from our friends, and we in turn are called to give care and support not only to family and friends, but also to all in need. Failure to live out this relational way of being leads inevitably to alienation. Such idolatry is overcome only by true worship, self-restraint, and discernment.

III. Body, Soul, and Personhood: The Openness and Communion of Human Life in God

21. *Embodied Beings, Human Rights and the Body, Body Transfigured and Sanctified*

Human beings are a complex unity of body and soul (or, as is sometimes affirmed, of body, soul, and spirit). Body and soul are deeply united and interwoven: different yet complementary, they constitute an integral organic whole, one total person. We are both meaning-bearing beings (beings with *logos*) and embodied beings (beings with *soma*). This means that our bodies are endowed with sacred value. This *embodiedness* of humanity is strongly affirmed by Paul: 'I appeal to you therefore … to present your bodies as a living sacrifice, holy and acceptable to God, which is your spiritual worship' (Rom 12.1). 'Glorify God in your body' (1 Cor 6.20). What we do with our bodies is of spiritual importance, for our bodies are essential elements of who we are. They are not to be treated as a commodity or utilized according to our sinful selfish desires.

We are invited to participate in the transformative love of God in Christ with our whole being: soul and body. In the words of St John Climacus, 'A man flooded with the love of God reveals in his body, as if in a mirror, a glory like that of Moses when he came face to face with God.'[10] The human person as a whole—soul and body—is called to sanctification. Christian anthropology rejects any dualism of soul over against body.

While soul and body are united, there is clearly a distinction between them. The soul is indeed not visible as *soul*. Yet our character and behaviour disclose our soul, our inner self, which the Christian tradition refers to as the heart (*kardia*) and which constitutes the core of our personhood. We are embodied meaning-producing beings. Thus our soul transcends our body, but it needs the body in order to remain expressive. We are called to bodily transfiguration, going beyond selfish identification with our body. We can make sacrifices through organ donation, but we can never exchange our body for another. A person's body may suffer mutilation and be broken and damaged, and this may deeply affect the total person; but at the same time the basic reality of personhood remains. The body may be augmented by biotechnology, or by medical intervention, and once more this may affect the total person; yet the continuity of personhood is not altogether broken. Diminishment or supplementation of what the body is or might achieve does not affect its irreducible worth for the person that we are. Even when our human bodies are gravely impaired, we do not cease to be fully human persons according to the image and likeness of God.

The body has inherent worth—ontological, functional, and social—as does the physical side of all things created. First, the body is an intrinsic aspect of our created nature. Second, the body is the necessary medium for the communication of meaning: being human always presupposes the body for transmission of sign, sound, and meaning. In the words of St Maximus the Confessor, the body is the 'messenger of the soul'.[11] Third, we are beings created according to the image of the Divine Logos, who reveals himself as incarnate, crucified, resurrected, and ascended to heaven in his glorified body.

Our embodiedness is a crucial element in our assertion of human rights. It is precisely because all humans, body and soul, are created by and for God that they must be protected from hunger and starvation and from all forms of abuse, such as torture, sexual violation, trafficking, and slavery.

22. *Struggle, Growth, and the Resurrection Body*

We suffer time's process of ageing, decay, and dissolution. Death is without doubt the sourest fruit of human disobedience (Gen 2.17), for it is radically contrary to God's intention. Nevertheless, 'we do not lose heart. Even though our outer nature is wasting away, our inner nature is being renewed day by day', by our life in the Spirit (2 Cor 4.16).

Despite these injurious consequences of sin, human beings have been given the ability to grow towards God, especially through the divine–human community of the Church as the Body of Christ. Indeed, this process of growth extends beyond the disintegration of the unity of body and soul at death, and embraces in hope their eventual reintegration at the Last Day. We look with hope 'for the resurrection of the dead and the life of the age to come' (Nicene-Constantinopolitan Creed).

Our bodies as well as our souls are subjected to the effects of sin. All constituents of the human being are disordered. Our spiritual struggle is not against the body but against sin. We do not seek to escape from the body, but we desire to be transfigured by conforming to the fullness of Christ: 'we wish not to be unclothed but to be further clothed, so that what is mortal may be swallowed up by life' (2 Cor 5.4). In this way, at the Last Day, we participate in the resurrection of both body and soul united as one total person before God and in his likeness. We look forward to a richer mode of existence in a body divinized or rendered 'spiritual' (1 Cor 15.44), in continuity with our expressive personality now, and yet endowed with a 'weight of glory' (2 Cor 4.17) far beyond our present experience.

Renewal and growth in the Spirit come through repentance, through the exercise of personal freedom, and, above all else, through the sacramental life and the salvation conferred upon all creation through the power of Christ's cross. For the way of the cross (Mk 8.34)—with all that it signifies: selflessness, humility, and love for God—is the path that leads to the resurrection of the whole person. In our Christian experience cross-bearing and resurrection are inseparable: 'dying, and see—we are alive' (2 Cor 6.9). We grow, not according to an obedience imposed moralistically, but through gladness and love evoked and given freely. We are called to change and grow in grace and faith, to become more Christ-like. Death can be accepted as a means of participating in the self-emptying of Christ. God in Christ allows us to experience the continuity of life, which is union with Christ, and thus to reverse death through death itself: 'Christ is risen from the dead, trampling down death by death, and upon those in the tombs bestowing life!' (Orthodox Paschal Hymn). Here, in the resurrection of Christ, is our answer to one of the most painful questions of the human being, the question of death.

23. *Gender, Difference, Relationship*

Being created according to the image and likeness of God entails both difference and relationship. Of primary importance is the difference between the creature and God the Creator. This is a fundamental difference of being. That is to say, the Creator surpasses the created order not by manner of place (*topos*) or degree, but by the order of nature (*physis*): God is uncreated and we are created.[12] Yet Christ as God meets us in the place of the created order, remaining uncreated at the same time.

Within the human race there is a basic difference between male and female: 'God created humankind in his image … male and female he created them' (Gen 1.27). While there is no gender or sexuality in God, our human gender—the distinction within humanity between male and female—is blessed by God. In virtue of the incarnation of God in Christ, gender difference, instead of being divisive, invites and presupposes relationship and unity, both to our Creator and to each other.

Our understanding of gender distinction must bear in mind the complex questions raised in the case of those for whom the differentiation between male and female is not experienced as clearly defined. The Church is called to offer appropriate pastoral care to all.

24. *Personhood and Community, Persons in Society and History*

Personhood is conferred on us by God as the core of our innermost identity. We are persons invested with names and faces. We are relational beings called first and foremost to give and receive love. This calling is much more than a moral capacity on our part. It is our very way of existence, for our personhood always presupposes the other person in order to fulfil itself in communion. As the ancient African concept of *ubuntu* ('I am because you are') affirms, and as much contemporary philosophy emphasizes, we discover the other as constitutive of our self-awareness as persons; we are essentially dialogical, interrelational, and dependent on the other. Theology understands this relationality precisely as a reflection of the divine image.

We are created according to the image of divine Trinitarian love. While there is a clear distinction between divine and human love, the fact that we are created according the image of divine Trinitarian love implies relation to others in accordance with their full worth. We discover that in our true selves we are intrinsically social beings, not merely self-sufficient individuals. This means that sociality and service are deeply attuned with our innermost being. Selfish individualism is, by contrast, a betrayal of our being as envisaged by God.

The social aspect of being human is revealed in and through history: we are historical beings. Just as the Holy Trinity has been revealed in time through the incarnation of the Son, so we humans find, create, and transmit meanings and values in and through time. This entails our responsibility to the past, present, and future. In the same way, Christian tradition is not an abstract conservation of static and given realities, but a creative development of our living experience. The ways in which Christians live their faith change over time as do the societies they affect. Time and space, along with the values we receive and create as social beings, are intrinsic to the created order. Differences with regard to language structures, to inherited customs, as well as to local sensitivities, mould human consciousness profoundly. Our cultural inheritance contains both positive and negative elements and must therefore be evaluated with critical appreciation. As creatures grounded in culture and history we are called in common to take prophetic and practical action in relation to the critical issues facing our societies.

25. *Marriage and Family*

Christ calls all men and women into a life of service according to their vocation. Though we are many and though we are called in many different ways, it is the one God who unites us all in the one Body of the Church. 'All these [gifts] are activated by one and the same Spirit, who allots to each one individually just as the Spirit chooses' (1 Cor 12.11). This can be seen when Jesus calls the apostles (Mt 4.18–22; Jn 1.43–48) and the rich youth (Mk 10.21), or when he invites the Virgin Mary to see St John as her son (Jn 19.26). Christ always allows for free decision and joyful acceptance of calling. All are called to a life in relationship, which may be expressed in different Spirit-filled ways: in particular, through marriage, through community life, whether monastic or lay, or through the single life.

While universal in its scope, and embracing all humankind, marriage has a particular significance for Christians. In a true marriage, according to God's will, the couple see God's glory reflected in one another's faces. Marriage, so Jesus states explicitly, reflects our original creation by God: 'He answered, "Have you not read that the one who made them at the beginning 'made them male and female', and said, 'For this reason a man shall leave his father and mother and be joined to his wife, and the two shall become one flesh'? So they are no longer two, but one flesh. Therefore what God has joined together, let no one separate"' (Mt 19.4–6). Christ's first miracle was performed at the wedding feast of Cana and thereby he gave his blessing to the union of marriage, endorsing the event of two persons, man and woman, joining in love (Jn 2.1–12).

The spiritual value of marriage is evident from the way in which Scripture uses it as an analogy for the relationship between God and his people (Hos 2.14–20; Song 2.8–13). More especially, the analogy describes the union between Christ and the Church: '"a man will leave his father and mother and be joined to his wife, and the two will become one flesh." This is a great mystery, and I am applying it to Christ and the church. Each of you, however, should love his wife as himself' (Eph 5.31–33). The love that husband and wife share with each other is here likened to the love of Christ towards the Church. This deeper sacramental meaning of marriage is particularly evident when the wedding service is celebrated together with the Eucharist.

The blessing of marriage is a celebration of the local Christian community as a whole. It is a sign of holy calling, a commitment within ongoing discipleship, as Christians grow more and more into the likeness of Christ. The Christian family is intimately embraced by the Church. St Augustine refers to the family as the 'domestic church' (*domestica ecclesia*),[13] and St John Chrysostom names the family as 'the little church' (*micra ecclesia*).[14] Like the Church itself, the family signifies relationship, both internally among its members, and externally in openness to all. Internally, it provides solidarity through mutual help and comfort between the family members, and externally it helps others through hospitality and practical support (1 Tim 5.8; Rom 16.4). Marriage is a blessing both upon the mutual love of the couple and, if it is the will of God, upon the procreation of children, who are regarded by the Church as a precious fruit of married life. In marriage man and woman join in God's own creative work.

For both Anglicans and Orthodox the sacrament of marriage involves lifelong commitment. However, marriage and family life, like all human relationships in a world distorted by sin, often fall short of the divine intention. Domestic violence, the emotional and physical abuse of children, and wilful neglect are all painful examples of this. So too are everyday failures in personal communication. The widespread breakdown of marriage, the increase of divorce and of single-parent families, and the transformation of working roles for parents have all placed marriage under grave pressure. Christians are called to support and uphold one another as we struggle with these challenges. Orthodox and most Anglicans agree that, under certain circumstances, the Church may allow remarriage after divorce.

For Christ Jesus the true family are those who do God's will: 'And he replied, "Who are my mother and my brothers?" And looking at those who sat around him, he said, "Here are my mother and my brothers! Whoever does the will of God is my brother and sister and mother"' (Mk 3.32–35). In this way Jesus himself offers a new understanding of family relationships. They serve as an expression of the ecclesial community, pointing towards the reign of God where they are transfigured.

26. *Monastic Life*

The monastic life—even the life of the solitary or hermit—no less than marriage, reflects the fullness of relational life in unconditional love, in regard both to God and to all the others around us. The monastic community may be seen as a Christian family of persons united in spiritual friendship through Christ by the Spirit. In such a family human relationships are transformed through the grace of the Kingdom. 'Jesus said, "Truly, I tell you, there is no one who has left house or brothers or sisters or mother or father or children or fields, for my sake and for the sake of the good news, who will not receive a hundredfold now in this age … and in the age to come eternal life"' (Mk 10.29–30). This type of communion often proves to be deeper and more meaningful than relations due to natural birth. However, in monastic life as in marital family life, Christ Jesus is to be loved above all else, for he is the one who loves us the most.

Monasticism provides a prophetic and eschatological witness to the age to come in which the state of marriage is transcended: 'Those who belong to this age marry and are given in marriage; but those who are considered worthy of a place in that age and in the resurrection from the dead neither marry nor are given in marriage' (Lk 20.34–35). The purpose of the monastic vocation is 'to make public, prophetic witness to the Christian hope of the Kingdom'.[15] At the same time, St John Chrysostom insists that the spiritual struggle is to be undertaken not only by monastics but by all the baptized: 'You greatly delude yourself and err, if you think that one thing is demanded from the layman and another from the monk; since the difference between them consists simply in the fact that one is married and the other is not, while in everything else they have the same responsibilities. All must rise to the same height.'[16] Some lay Christians, particularly but not exclusively in the West, are drawn to forms of 'intentional community'. Such communities, often with a rule of life, seek to serve God's Kingdom in a variety of ways, through prayer, study, and hospitality and in responding to human need.

Within monasticism, especially in the Christian East, a central role is played by the ministry of the spiritual father (*geron*, *starets*) and spiritual mother (*gerontissa*, *staritsa*). In both Eastern and Western monasticism this ministry is often fulfilled by the abbot or abbess. The spiritual father or mother, invested with special blessings by the Spirit, adopts the monk or nun into Christ as a spiritual son or daughter. In both East and West, those who are not monastics, whether married or single, may likewise place themselves under the guidance of a spiritual mother or father. In the Western Celtic tradition the spiritual guide is sometimes called a 'soul friend' (*anam cara*). In the Anglican tradition patterns of spiritual direction and accompaniment are becoming increasingly prevalent. Alongside spiritual fatherhood and motherhood there exists also the creative relationship of spiritual brotherhood and sisterhood.

27. *The Single Life*

Besides the life of marriage and the life of monastic celibacy there is another possibility: the single life, which also is blessed by God. Many discover the fulfilment of non-monastic, celibate life as their lifelong calling. In some cases the single life will have been deliberately embraced, as a result of mature and considered choice. In the case of others who find themselves single, this is not through choice. Such persons may be able to transform what could be seen as an unwanted circumstance into a positive vocation that is genuinely relational and outreaching, and a great blessing to the life of the Church.

28. *Friendship*

Our creation in the image and likeness of the triune God, as persons intended for a life of relationship and love, implies friendship. Friendship is a special kind of relationship, often unlinked to any specific task or social role or function. At its heart is the simple enjoyment of the company of the other, of the conversation and exchange between two or more people. Such relationships may inspire profound loyalty and lead to a deepening of understanding and to spiritual growth. 'Some friends play at friendship but a true friend sticks closer than one's nearest kin' (Prov 18.24). Friendship is universal and may be seen as incarnated equally in the ways of life given in marriage, in monasticism, or in the single life. The far-reaching value of friendship is evident in the distress and suffering caused by its breakdown or betrayal, or by the loss of a friend through illness and death. There is no friendship in the abstract; friendship presupposes a personal relationship with someone specific. Spiritual friendship is a crucial way of being human, especially needed in our contemporary culture marked by fragmentation and loneliness. We have as a notable example the spiritual friendship forged between St John Chrysostom and St Olympias.[17]

God is the ever-faithful, life-giving friend of every human person. The more we experience God's friendship, and the more we realize how dear we are to God, the more we recognize our creatureliness and dependence. Just as Abraham is called 'the friend of God' (Jas 2.23: cf. 2 Chron 20.7 and Isa 41.8), so also each one of us is the friend of God. Jesus displayed overflowing friendship towards all. The Orthodox Church refers to him as *Philanthropos*, the friend of all humankind. One striking example of his friendship is seen in the story of Mary, Martha, and Lazarus. Jesus referred to Lazarus specifically as 'our friend' (*philos*)

(Jn 11.11), and such was his feeling for his friend that he wept at his graveside, leading the Jews to exclaim 'See how he loved him!' (Jn 11.35–36). It is noteworthy that our Lord linked friendship with sacrifice and obedience: 'love one another as I have loved you. No one has greater love than this, to lay down one's life for one's friends. You are my friends if you do what I command you' (Jn 15.12–14). Friendship replaces servitude in the new community: 'I do not call you servants any longer … but I have called you friends, because I have made known to you everything that I have heard from my Father' (Jn 15.15). As St Aelred of Rievaulx writes: 'God is friendship' (*Deus amicitia est*) ... he who abides in friendship abides in God, and God in him.'[18] Friendship with God inspires awe and devotion and it causes the divine light to shine forth in our persons as images of God.

29. *Value of the Human Person in All Stages of Life*

Christianity affirms the intrinsic value of the human person from the beginning to the end of life.

Children constitute an important part in the life of the Church and the world. From the beginning Christianity was a faith preached to the young. Christ taught us that children are precious and valuable and that they should not be hindered. The Kingdom of God belongs to children and to those who, although no longer children, remain like them in virtue of their simplicity, sense of wonder, and undivided joy: 'Let the little children come to me; do not stop them; for it is to such as these that the kingdom of God belongs' (Mk 10.14). Should not these virtues of children enhance all the later stages of life, from youth to middle age to old age?

Youth offers an enthusiasm and vitality that should never be underestimated or marginalized (see 1 Tim 4.12). Among Christ's disciples who transformed the world, some were young. Young people worldwide represent a transformative potential of the highest order. But youthfulness is not determined by biological age alone, for purity of heart is what makes us spiritually youthful.

Middle age, as a point of transition and sometimes of crisis, offers the opportunity to grow in self-exploration and insight. It adds responsibility to strength; it adds experience to leadership.

Despite the limitations and fragility that old age often brings, the elderly are of inestimable value. A society is gravely impoverished when it does not appreciate the wisdom and dignity of its older members.

All generations are called to share in the plan of God's love by reciprocally exchanging the gifts with which each person is endowed. In this way all the cycles of life express our personhood, bringing forth the inner riches of our human potential. Nevertheless, while it is important to recognize the different gifts which people at all stages of life bring to society, we strongly affirm that the essential dignity of the person is not dependent on such contributions.

30. *The Dignity of Human Nature*

Human dignity is given by God. Each human person is of absolute worth and is to be treated always as an end, not a means. In a globalized culture, with its powerful mass movements and the danger of domination by technology, it is vitally important to insist upon the supreme value of each human person. Scripture consistently alerts us to the dangers of becoming conformed to the 'powers and principalities' of the world, the 'cosmic powers' or 'spiritual forces of evil' (Eph 6.12). We are summoned to 'stand firm' (Gal 5.1) in the freedom that Christ has given us. The lordship of Christ is a critique of the many lordships claiming our obedience, politically, culturally, or economically.

Protecting the intrinsic worth of each and every human being needs to be regarded as an obligation of the first order. We are called to support and protect the rights of all who are vulnerable, the refugee, the homeless, the orphan, the infirm, and the bereaved, and to ensure that all are provided with care, food, shelter, and clothing, and not left at risk of injury or death from neglect.

Something new, something long hoped for, arrives in Christ Jesus and his ministry, as he reaches out in love against all manner of negations of God's good creation and purpose. The Christian vocation to follow Jesus includes acting with love in every society regardless of its political structure or legal system. The Church as the Body of Christ bears witness that all human beings made in the image and likeness of God, restored in the death and resurrection of Christ, are to become bearers of God's Kingdom of justice and righteousness. Some areas of particular relevance are environmental and economic justice, regard for the rule of law, respect for the sanctity of life, and the elimination of slavery and human trafficking. In particular, our personal responsibility includes engagement in conflict resolution and peacemaking. Following Christ who reconciled us to himself (2 Cor 5.18; Rom 11.15), we are ourselves called to be ministers of reconciliation (2 Cor 5.18–19), critically challenging every system that is violent, oppressive, and opposed to peace and justice. The redeeming work of Christ, however, is not to be equated with any political ideology. Socio-political action, while essential, cannot save us of itself, neither can it provide us with victory over death.

Disengagement or despair is not a Christian option. We claim the right to bear witness openly to our faith and to speak for the ways of Jesus Christ in all human affairs, acting as the salt of the earth and the light of the world (Mt 5.13–14). This necessarily includes a commitment to ensuring the fundamental right of all people freely to practise their religion. We gratefully recognize the contribution of all those who, whether members of the Church or not, are working for the aims of the Kingdom, and it is our desire to cooperate in active partnership with them.

31. *God-Given Freedom: Formal Freedom of Choice and Substantial Freedom in and for God*

Freedom is an essential aspect of the divine image in humankind. As God is free, so the human being, in his image, is also free. God's freedom is absolute and unlimited, whereas our human freedom is limited in many ways: by heredity, environment, and sin, whether original or personal. Yet freedom remains always an inalienable part of true personhood.

There is a distinction to be made between the dignity of human *nature* (the capacity for personal freedom as such) and the dignity expressed in a person's *life* (the actual living out of freedom through spiritual and moral good). There are two modes of freedom. One mode, formal freedom, is the capacity for self-governance through the ability to choose: for example, between different courses of action. Such ability to choose is innate to every human being and, while it can be reduced or distorted, it can never be totally destroyed, for it pertains to the *image*. The second mode is freedom understood as liberation from sin. This is the freedom to cooperate in obedience with God's love. Hence freedom for God in grace is an expression of *substantial* freedom. It is the freedom which Jesus Christ restores to us through Baptism and reaffirms in Eucharistic communion: 'So if the Son makes you free, you will be free indeed' (Jn 8.36). In this way it pertains to the *likeness*.

The fact that we humans are endowed with freedom means that every human person lives out the image and likeness of God in his or her unique and distinctive way. There are as many different ways of loving and serving God as there are different human persons. The variety and complexity of human beings are well expressed in two Jewish sayings: 'God never does the same thing twice', and 'the world has need of every single human person'.

Any discussion of human freedom must always take full account of divine grace. Anglicans often use the Pauline language of justification by grace through faith, and sanctification or growth in holiness as we walk in the Spirit. Orthodox emphasize the presence of the Holy Spirit and the agency of the energies (*energeiai*) of the one triune God, whom we come to know in Christ. Despite certain differences of emphasis, the two traditions are in fundamental agreement. Anglicans and Orthodox affirm that it is only by the grace of God that true freedom in Christ may be attained.

32. *From Freedom to Glory*

Our right use of freedom, our pilgrimage from image to likeness, our membership of the mystical Body of Christ, all point towards the completion of our human nature and the transformation of all creation on the Last Day. This is our true fulfilment, the ultimate joy of all creation, our eternal sharing in the Trinitarian life of love. Advancing from glory to glory (2 Cor 3.18), we never cease to grow in wonderment at the divine beauty. This final glory exceeds our imagination. Our desire and longing for this are affirmed whenever we pray, 'Our Father in heaven, hallowed be your name, your kingdom come. Your will be done, on earth as it is in heaven' (Mt 6.9–10).

We are baptized into the saving death of the Lord, and we will rise with him in newness of life. For 'He is the head of the body, the Church; he is the beginning, the firstborn from the dead, so that he might come to have first place in everything. For in him all the fullness of God was pleased to dwell, and through him God was pleased to reconcile to himself all things, whether on earth or in heaven, by making peace through the blood of his cross' (Col 1.18–20).

'To the one seated on the throne and to the Lamb be blessing and honour and glory and might for ever and ever!' (Rev 5.13). Such is the vision of the end of history in the Revelation to John. Evil is destroyed, all is completed, God will be 'all in all' (1 Cor 15.28). God who created us in wonderful diversity will keep us to all eternity, each in our unique personhood.

A Hymn of Glory to the Trinity

Glory to God the Father
And to the Son who reigns over all.
Glory to the Spirit, All-Holy,
To whom praise is fitting.
This is the Single God, the Trinity,
Who created all things that are;
Who filled the heavens with spiritual beings,
The land with earthly creatures,
The oceans, rivers, springs,
With all aquatic living things.
Out of his own Spirit he gives life
to all that lives

So that all created life can sing out praise
To the wisdom of the Maker;
That single cause of their existence,
Their continuing subsistence.

But more than all other things,
Rational nature must sing out
That he is the Great King, Good Father.
And so, my Father, grant to me
In spirit and in soul, in heart and voice,
In purity of heart
To give you the glory. Amen.

St Gregory of Nazianzus, *Hymn* I, 1.31, Patrologia Graeca 37, 510–11 (tr. John A. McGuckin)

So if anyone is in Christ, there is a new creation: everything old has passed away; see, everything has become new! All this is from God, who reconciled us to himself through Christ, and has given us the ministry of reconciliation; that is, in Christ God was reconciling the world to himself, not counting their trespasses against them, and entrusting the message of reconciliation to us.

2 Cor 5.17–19

Notes

1. *On the Incarnation*, 54.
2. *Against Heresies*, III, 21, 9.
3. *Against Heresies,* IV, 20, 7
4. *The Moscow Agreed Statement,* III, 9; cf *The Dublin Agreed Statement*, III, 49.
5. Collect for Peace, Morning Prayer, *Book of Common Prayer.*
6. *Akathist to the Holy Virgin*, Ikos 1.3-8, 1.10-13.
7. Compare with the title of the report of the Anglican–Roman Catholic International Commission, *Mary: Grace and Hope in Christ* (ed. D Bolen, G Cameron. Continuum Books, London 2006).
8. *Book of Difficulties*, 7
9. *Scientific Autobiography and Other Papers*, tr. F. Gaynor (London: Williams and Norgate Ltd., 1950), 184. Translation modified.
10. *The Ladder of Divine Ascent*, Step 30, Patrologia Graeca 88, 1157B. Cf. Exodus 34.30..

11. *Exposition of the Lord's Prayer*, Corpus Christianorum: Series Graeca, 23, 62-63, 619-625.

12. St John of Damascus, *An Exact Exposition of the Orthodox Faith*, I, 13, Patrologia Graeca 94, 853C.

13. *On the Good of Widowhood*, Patrologia Latina 40, 450.

14. *Homily XX on Ephesians*, Patrologia Graeca 62, 143A..

15. Community of the Resurrection, 'Prologue', in *Constitutions* (Mirfield: Community of the Resurrection, 1991).

16. *To the Faithful Father*, 3, 14, Patrologia Graeca 47, 372–4.

17. St John Chrysostom, *Letters to Olympias* I-XVII. Also see *The Life of Olympias*, 5, 6, 8.

18. *Spiritual Friendship (Kalamazoo: Cistercian Publications, 1977), 26.*6

Membership of the International Commission 2009–15

Representatives of the Orthodox Church

Ecumenical Patriarchate

Metropolitan Kallistos of Diokleia (Co-Chairman) 2009–15

Patriarchate of Alexandria

Metropolitan Seraphim of Johannesburg 2010–15

Patriarchate of Antioch

The Revd Fr Alexander Haig 2009–15

Patriarchate of Jerusalem

The Revd Dr George Dion Dragas 2009, 2010, 2015

The Revd Archimandrite Aristovoulos Kyriazis 2014

Patriarchate of Moscow

The Revd Dr Kirill Hovorun 2009, 2010, 2011

Archbishop Elisey of Sourozh 2012

The Revd Fr Valentin Vasechko 2013–15

Patriarchate of Serbia

Dr Bogdan Lubardic 2009–15

Patriarchate of Romania

Metropolitan Nifon of Târgovişte 2009–15

Patriarchate of Georgia

Bishop Melkhisedek of Herety 2009

The Revd Dr Giorgi Zviadadze 2009, 2010

Mr David Chanadiri 2012

Church of Cyprus

Metropolitan Chrysostomos of Kition 2009–15

Church of Greece

Professor Dr Miltiadis Konstantinou 2010–15

Co-Secretary

The Revd Dr Christos B. Christakis 2009–15

Church of Albania

Bishop Ilia of Philomelion 2009–15

Church of Poland

The Revd Andrzej Minko 2011, 2013

Representatives of the Anglican Communion

Archbishop Roger Herft

(The Anglican Church of Australia) 2009–15

(Co-Chairman)

The Revd Dr Timothy Bradshaw

(The Church of England) 2009–15

(Acting Co-Secretary 2009)

The Most Revd Richard Clarke

(The Church of Ireland) 2011–15

The Revd Dr Thomas Ferguson

(The Episcopal Church) [USA] 2009

The Revd Canon Jonathan Goodall

(Archbishop of Canterbury's Representative) 2009, 2010, 2011, 2013

Bishop William Gregg

(The Episcopal Church) [USA] 2009

The Revd Canon Deacon Dr Christine Hall

(The Church of England) 2009–15

The Revd Canon Philip Hobson OGS

(The Anglican Church of Canada) 2009–15

The Revd Dr Gloria Mapangdol

(The Episcopal Church in the Philippines) 2010–15

Ms Natasha Klukach

(The Anglican Church of Canada) 2009–15

Bishop Michael Lewis

(The Episcopal Church in Jerusalem and the Middle East) 2009–15

The Revd Dr Duncan Reid

(The Anglican Church of Australia) 2009–15

The Revd Canon Professor John Riches

(Scottish Episcopal Church) 2009–15

Bishop John Stroyan

(The Church of England) 2009–15

The Revd Marc Billimoria

(Church of Ceylon) 2012–15

The Revd Joseph Wandera

(The Anglican Church of Kenya) 2009, 2013

The Revd Canon Dr Alyson Barnett-Cowan

(Co-Secretary) 2010–14

The Revd Canon Dr John Gibaut

(Co-Secretary) 2015

The Revd Neil Vigers

(Staff—Anglican Communion Office) 2009–15

Members of the Commission outside the Orthodox Church of the Annunciation in Buffalo, September 2015